American Moments

ABDO
Daughters

THE CALIFORNIA GOLD RUSH

By Sheila Rivera

VISIT US AT
WWW.ABDOPUB.COM

Published by ABDO Publishing Company, 4940 Viking Drive, Suite 622, Edina, Minnesota 55435. Copyright ©2004 by Abdo Consulting Group, Inc. International copyrights reserved in all countries. No part of this book may be reproduced in any form without written permission from the publisher.

Printed in the United States.

Edited by: Cory Gunderson
Contributing Editor: Tamara L. Britton
Interior Production and Design: Terry Dunham Incorporated
Cover Design: Mighty Media
Photos: Corbis, Library of Congress

Library of Congress Cataloging-in-Publication Data

Rivera, Sheila, 1970-
    California gold rush / Sheila Rivera.
        p. cm. -- (American moments)
    Includes index.
    Summary: Discusses the early history of California, focusing especially on the gold rush period including the discovery of gold, the arrival of prospectors hoping to strike it rich, and the effects on the people and environment of the region.
    ISBN 1-59197-281-7
    1. California--Gold discoveries--Juvenile literature. 2. Gold mines and mining--California--History--19th century--Juvenile literature. 3. Frontier and pioneer life--California--Juvenile literature. 4. California--History--1846-1850--Juvenile literature. [1. California--Gold discoveries. 2. California--History--1846-1850. 3. Frontier and pioneer life--California.] I. Title. II. Series.

F865.R63 2004
979.4'04--dc21
                                                                2003050307

CONTENTS

CALIFORNIA'S EARLY HISTORY

In 1533, a Spanish adventurer named Hernán Cortés was in present-day Mexico with a group of explorers. At that time, the Spanish controlled Mexico. They called it New Spain. Cortés sent a group of explorers north. They traveled by ship along Mexico's western coast.

Cortés was looking for a legendary waterway called the Strait of Anián. It was supposed to be a sea route through North and South America to Asia. The Europeans often traded goods and services in Asia. But to get there, Europeans had to travel south around South America. The Strait of Anián would provide a shortcut.

The expedition that Cortés had sent north was led by Captain Diego de Becerra. During the voyage, a man named Fortún Jiménez led a revolt on the ship. Becerra was killed in the revolt. Jiménez and his crew took control of the ship and continued on their journey.

The expedition landed at La Paz Bay, which was on the Baja California Peninsula. When they landed, Jiménez and 22 of his men went ashore. They were later killed by the local Guaycura Indians. Only two of Jiménez's men survived the attacks.

Upon hearing news of the disaster, Cortés led a second expedition north from Acapulco in 1535. The group traveled to the same peninsula. It landed in La Paz Bay and built a base there.

The base became a home for the Spaniards. From there they were able to explore more of the land. Cortés remained in the settlement until 1536.

Spaniards continued to explore the region. On June 27, 1542, a man named Juan Rodríguez Cabrillo set sail from Mexico with another group of explorers. They headed toward California. This group, too, went in search of the Strait of Anián. The expedition landed in San Diego Bay on September 28, 1542. This was the first time that Europeans set foot on the land that is now known as California.

The Spanish explorers never found the Strait of Anián. Despite the rocky results of the initial expeditions, European interest in California continued. In 1769, California became a colonial province of Spain. The Spanish wanted to bring Christianity to the people living in California. They built numerous missions along the coast between San Diego and San Francisco.

The first nine missions were founded by Junípero Serra. Serra was a Spanish Franciscan monk. He arrived in California in 1769. He became father-president of the growing mission system. When

Hernán Cortés

Serra died, he was replaced by Fermín Francisco de Lasuen. Lasuen doubled the number of missions in this new territory. The Spanish considered the missions both important and successful.

A map of early Christian missions in California

At the missions, local Native Americans learned about the Christian religion. In addition, they learned to become successful traders in the new Spanish society. They were expected to adapt to the changing world around them.

However, some Native Americans were hostile toward the new Spanish presence. They did not like the missions or the invaders settling on their land. Sometimes they attacked the missions.

In order to protect themselves, the Spanish built four military forts on the California coast. These forts were called presidios. From there, soldiers worked to keep the missionaries safe. However, the Spanish soldiers needed supplies, and they needed them right away.

The presidios' locations made it easy for the Spanish to bring supplies to the forts by water. So, supplies that could be shipped by boat arrived quickly. However, there was not enough food in the new territory to feed all of the soldiers. The Spanish believed they could solve this problem by bringing more people to the region. These people would set up farms and shops, which could feed and supply the soldiers. But, the Spanish government would have to work to get people to come to the new land.

The government's plan to draw new settlers to California involved several steps. First, towns were built throughout the colony. Second, the government offered people free livestock, land, farming equipment, clothing, and other supplies if they would agree to settle in California. Third, the government pledged not to collect taxes from new settlers during the first five years that they lived there. The offer seemed attractive, but there was a catch. The settlers had to promise to sell any extra crops they raised to the forts for the soldiers.

Many people took advantage of this opportunity and came to California. In 1777, the city of San Jose was established. Los Angeles followed shortly afterward in 1781. The Spanish communities were beginning to boom, just as the government had hoped. However, California would not be under Spanish control for much longer.

The Presidio, built in 1776 by Spanish soldiers to guard the entrance of San Francisco Bay, is the longest-serving military base in the United States. The fort was one of four presidios built along the California coast.

In 1821, Mexico and Spain signed the Treaty of Córdoba. Under the treaty, Mexico became an independent nation. California remained a northern province of Mexico. The change of government from Spanish to Mexican was hard on the Christian missions in California. Under the Mexican government, missions lost most of their power and land. Most of the mission land was used for cattle ranches.

Later, more and more American settlers moved into California. The first wagon trains of settlers arrived in 1841. As more people moved to California, the United States became more interested in acquiring it from Mexico.

A map of the western United States and northern Mexico in 1846

In 1846, the United States and Mexico went to war. The U.S. government offered many reasons for the war. Mexicans had attacked U.S. citizens and property. So, the U.S. government believed that the Mexican government owed it money. In addition, Mexico owed England money and the United States thought that Mexico might give up the land in order to pay its debt.

On the other side of the argument, the Mexican government was angry because of U.S. involvement in Texas. A decade earlier, Texas had been part of Mexico. Texas declared its independence and fought to be free from Mexican control. Texas won its freedom and became an independent country. The United States had supported Texas in its war with Mexico. Texas later became a part of the United States, which further angered the Mexican government.

The Mexicans won minor victories in the Mexican War. But the United States won the major battles and eventually the war. It ended in 1848, when both sides signed the Treaty of Guadalupe Hidalgo. The treaty gave the United States control of California. California would never fall under Mexican control again.

THE ALAMO

The cry of "Remember the Alamo" inspired Texans in their fight for independence from Mexico. The Alamo was a former Spanish mission where a small number of Texans made a stand against Mexican general Antonio López de Santa Anna's army. On March 6, 1836, the 13-day siege ended when Mexican soldiers stormed the Alamo's walls and overwhelmed the defenders. The battle claimed the lives of 189 Texan and American fighters.

The Alamo in San Antonio, Texas

A battle scene from the Mexican War

A border dispute between the United States and Mexico led to the Mexican War. The United States insisted the Rio Grande marked the border between Texas and Mexico. Mexico maintained that the Nueces River formed the border. In May 1846, fighting broke out. The United States captured the northern Mexican province of California. In September 1847, U.S. forces entered Mexico City. By winning the war, the United States acquired territory from Mexico that would become all or part of Arizona, California, Colorado, Nevada, New Mexico, Utah, and Wyoming.

DISCOVERY OF GOLD

One of California's most influential people at this time was a man named John A. Sutter. Sutter, the son of Swiss parents, was born in Baden, Germany, in 1803. After falling into terrible debt, he moved to New York in 1834 to rebuild his life. Sutter left his family in Germany with his brother. But he was not happy or successful in New York. Sutter decided that the West offered him more opportunity, so he moved from New York to Missouri. He worked there for three years as a trader on the Santa Fe Trail.

In 1838, Sutter decided that Mexican-controlled California offered him the greatest chance of success. He traveled west along a path called the Oregon Trail. Sutter followed it until he came to Fort Vancouver, near what is now Portland, Oregon. From there, he headed south to California.

Sutter finally arrived in California in 1839. He soon met with the provincial governor of California in Monterey. Sutter talked to him about building a colony there. The governor agreed, and gave Sutter nearly 50,000 acres (20,000 ha) of land to build the colony.

On part of this land, Sutter built Sutter's Fort between 1840 and 1842. It became the home of his business. The California government wanted Sutter to use his fort to stop any threat that might come. Threats to California settlers included robberies, invasions

Sutter's Fort was founded in 1841. The discovery of gold on Sutter's property started the California gold rush.

by Native Americans, and the hunting and trapping of animals by foreign companies.

The fort was built near a river Sutter called the American River. This site on the Sacramento River was close to what is now the city of Sacramento. Once completed, the fort's adobe walls were massive. They were 18 feet (5 m) high and three feet (1 m) thick. Sutter's settlement began to grow.

John Sutter

Sutter acquired another nearby fort, Fort Ross, from a group of Russians in 1841. The Russians had used Fort Ross as a base camp while they worked as fur traders, trapping wild animals and selling their furs for money. By the 1840s, trapping had become unprofitable. The fur hats that had been in style in Europe were no longer popular. So fur was not as valuable as it once had been. In addition, it had become more difficult for trappers to find the animals. The poor economic times in the fur trade business forced some Russians to leave the area.

As the Russians left, they offered to sell the fort to Sutter for $30,000. Sutter gave them a note promising to pay them, but he never did. After the Russians left, he took the fort apart. He moved all of its equipment, livestock, and goods to Sutter's Fort in the Sacramento Valley.

By 1844, Sutter's Fort had become a center for trade in California. Many travelers came to the fort, and Sutter welcomed them all. Immigrants from the United States were a big source of trade to the fort. They also protected Sutter's Fort when the Mexican War began. U.S. soldiers did not attack the fort because so many Americans lived inside.

Many of the people who lived in the fort worked for Sutter. He employed between 100 and 500 people. These employees included blacksmiths, carpenters, farmers, gardeners, gunsmiths, hunters, sheepherders, tanners, and trappers. He also employed weavers, millwrights, and a distiller.

Sutter's employees used large quantities of wood to make buildings and products. To fulfill the employees' need for wood, Sutter sent search teams to find a good place to build a sawmill. The sawmill would be used to process trees into the lumber that Sutter needed at the fort.

Sutter hoped that a sawmill could be built on the American River. Then the wood could be rafted down the river to his fort. This plan was supposed to permanently meet the lumber needs of Sutter's Fort. Instead, it created more problems than Sutter could ever have anticipated.

Sutter's Fort and Sutter's Mill were located along the Sacramento and American rivers.

James Marshall, a carpenter, had been hired by Sutter to build the mill. On January 24, 1848, Marshall was working at the nearly completed sawmill when he stumbled upon a shiny stone in the water. Upon finding the stone of gold, Marshall remarked, "Boys, by God, I believe I have found a gold mine." He rushed the stone back to Sutter. After checking his encyclopedia, Sutter determined that the substance was indeed gold.

What seemed like a happy moment for the men soon turned sour. Sutter worried that the discovery of gold would bring mobs of people to the area. He did not want people on his land hunting for gold. So, Sutter asked all of his employees to keep the find a secret. Yet within a few months the word was out, and hoards of people came.

As more and more people came to California, things grew worse for Sutter. When the Mexican War ended and California fell under U.S. control, Sutter lost all legal rights to his land.

By this time, word of the gold discovery had spread throughout the city of San Francisco and on through the entire nation. On December 5, 1848, U.S. president James K. Polk formally announced that gold had been found in California. Polk's announcement inspired what is believed to be one of the largest human migrations in American history.

Before the discovery of gold, California's non-native population had been around 14,000. In two years' time, 40,000 people moved to California. By 1852, the state's population was 250,000. Travelers stormed over Sutter's land. They destroyed his crops and killed his livestock for food.

Sutter spent the rest of his life in court, battling the state of California and the U.S. federal government. He felt that the government owed him money for the damage done to his land by the gold hunters. Sutter never collected all of his money. He died in Washington DC in 1880.

Opposite page: *James Marshall discovers gold at Sutter's Mill.*

FORTY-NINERS

People came to California from everywhere in search of gold. Most had the simple dream of making a better life for themselves. They believed that the wealth they would find in California would help them reach this goal.

One miner, Melvin Paden, wrote his wife a letter, describing such a hope. He wrote, "Jane, I left you and the boys for no other reason than this: To come here and procure a little property by the sweat of my brow so that we could have a place of our own, that I might not be a dog for other people any longer."

In 1849 alone, 100,000 people came to California. The newspapers spread stories of gold "collected at random and without any trouble." Even President Polk endorsed California's riches. In a meeting with Congress, Polk discussed "the accounts of the abundance of gold." People took the president's words as the truth. Those who heard Polk were very excited about the gold in California. They wanted it for themselves. Many people were willing to travel long distances to get it.

James K. Polk

Panning for gold

ANOTHER GOLD RUSH

AUSTRALIA

The California gold rush played a role in another gold rush a world away. An Australian man named Edward Hargraves searched for gold in California in 1850. He was unsuccessful. The California goldfields reminded him of land in southeast Australia. He returned to Australia and discovered gold there in 1851. Hargraves's discovery triggered Australia's gold rush.

The new immigrants were called forty-niners. They got this name because most began their journeys to California in the year 1849. Anyone who arrived between 1849 and 1852 was called a forty-niner.

Forty-niners came from as far away as Australia, China, France, Germany, Mexico, New Zealand, the Hawaiian Islands, and Turkey. The voyage across the ocean was typically easier than the journey across land.

Treasure hunters from the United States came to California along three main routes. One route brought travelers from the East Coast by sea. The trip involved sailing around Cape Horn, at the southern tip of South America. This journey was 17,000 miles (27,359 km) long, and it often took more than six months to complete. Even though it was a long journey, many people traveled this route to California.

Soon, a second sea route was created that made the journey shorter. Gold hunters from the eastern United States sailed south to Panama, in Central America. The Panama Canal had not yet been built, so passengers left the ships and traveled across Panama. Once they reached the western side of the country, they boarded other ships to complete their journey north to California.

This trip was more expensive than sailing around South America. There were other drawbacks as well. Those who traveled through Panama often became sick with malaria or cholera. When they

Immigrants traveling across the United States to seek gold in California

reached the western side of Panama, ships were not always waiting there. The ships that took the treasure seekers to California didn't come very often. Sometimes these people had to wait weeks or months for the next ship to arrive.

Other travelers used a third route. They crossed the Great Plains of the United States. People who traveled this land route came on foot, on horseback, or by covered wagon. They stopped in Independence, Missouri, the last town before crossing the wilderness to California.

From Independence, the journey to Yuba County, California, was 2,000 miles (3,219 km). Along the trail, travelers faced rough terrain, scarce water, and dangerous Native Americans. Snow and harsh winter weather were hard on the travelers. Some of them died.

Men made up most of the travelers to California. Most women and children remained at home in the East, waiting for their husbands and fathers to return. Every year, an average of 30,000 people left California and returned home. However, 30,000 was a tiny number compared to the huge numbers that were coming in. California's population still continued its rapid growth.

The city of San Francisco grew more than most other cities in California. During the 1840s, before gold was discovered, San Francisco's population was only a few hundred people. Its population grew constantly after the discovery of gold. San Francisco's population grew from 800 to 50,000 in only a few years. During this time, an average of 30 new houses were built in San Francisco every day. Land that had sold for $16 in 1847, before the gold rush, was sold for $45,000 just 18 months later.

The discovery of gold in San Francisco led to a population explosion in the early 1850s.

Some of the biggest contributors to the population increase were Chinese immigrants. The first Chinese people came to California in February 1848. There were only three of them, two men and one woman. By January 1850, there were 791 Chinese immigrants living in California. All but two of them were men. By 1880, Chinese workers made up 22 percent of California's miners.

Life for the Chinese was difficult. Many never found gold, and they were forced into the backbreaking labor of building railroads. They were also forced to pay taxes because of their immigrant status.

When the gold rush was over, many Chinese people remained in California. They helped build additional railroads later in the century. The large number of international immigrants during the gold rush is one of the reasons why California's population is so diverse today.

A Chinese immigrant makes his way to the California gold mines.

American Moments

TOOLS OF THE TRADE

When the travelers finally made it to California, they went to work looking for gold. At the beginning of the gold rush there was a tremendous amount of gold, so it was relatively easy to find. Miners used a variety of tools to find gold. Each year, miners created new tools that would make their job easier. As gold became harder to find, the types of tools miners used became more specialized.

The main tools in any miner's equipment bag were a pick and a shovel. A pick is a tool shaped like a T. Its blade has a sharp point at each end. Miners used the pick to break rock away from the earth. The shovel was used afterward to move dirt away from the site of the dig.

One of the most common ways gold seekers found gold was by panning in the rivers. Miners used round, flat-bottomed pans with slanted sides. They looked like pie plates, or bowls. Miners filled their pans with dirt and

A miner holds a pan.

A mining pick and a shovel

water from the river's bottom. They swirled the water and dirt
around in the pans. Any gold nuggets would remain at the bottom
of the pans, while the water washed the dirt away. Panning was hard
on the miners. Working in the cold water all day left many of
them with sore backs, frozen feet, and tired knees.

Many miners became disgruntled by the hard work of panning.
So, they developed a new method of panning using a tool called a
cradle, or rocker. It looked like a baby's cradle. At least two
people were needed to operate a rocker. The first person's job was

Miners use a rocker to search for gold.

to dump water and dirt from the river into the rocker. The second person's job was to shake the rocker back and forth. The bottom of the rocker had bars, called rails, through which the water and dirt could fall. The water would wash the dirt through the railed bottom, leaving behind only the heaviest materials. These included rocks and, more importantly, gold.

From the rocker, miners advanced to a tool called a long tom, or a sluice box. A long tom was a long wooden tub. River water ran through the inside. Miners threw dirt into the tom and the water washed it away. Gold was too heavy for the water to wash out of the long tom. It sank to the bottom of the tom to be retrieved by the miners.

In time, the long tom was no longer useful. Gold had become harder to find. Miners had to be more creative. They turned to a new method of mining, using what they called coyote holes. Miners dug cavelike holes into the sides of ditches and hills. Dirt was hauled out so the miners could look for gold inside of the holes. This made the holes unstable, and many caved in on the miners inside. Despite the danger, many coyote holes were dug during this time.

During the 1850s, gold had become too hard to find using the usual methods. The gold that remained was deep inside the earth. Getting it out would be expensive. Most miners did not have the funds to do this. So big companies went to work to get the remaining gold.

Companies began to use waterpower to search for gold. This new process was called hydraulic mining. Water was channeled from rivers toward the sides of cliffs. Metal nozzles shot the water at the cliffs' sides, like old-fashioned water cannons. The water knocked the gravel, with gold inside, to the ground. The gravel then fell into strainers that separated it from the gold. These water cannons were extremely powerful. Water came out of them with such force that it could kill a person standing as far as 200 feet (61 m) away. As much as 5,000 tons (4,500 t) of gravel was washed away from cliffs every day from hydraulic mining.

The federal government banned hydraulic mining in 1884. The practice was harming rivers. But the method had been very profitable. By the time it was stopped, hydraulic mining had resulted in the discovery of more than $100 million in gold. That was one-third of all the gold discovered during the gold rush.

In the end, very few of the thousands of miners who traveled to California to find gold actually became rich. Many had planned to make a fortune in a matter of days. Instead, most spent months or even years working hard with little results.

As time wore on, miners became frustrated. They were angry that they hadn't found gold. Many began to think that other miners were taking all of it. Bitterness soon developed between miners, which led to fighting, theft, and murder. Jails became necessary in the mining communities. Government officials began hanging the worst criminals. The heyday of gold mining in California had come to an end.

Opposite page: *A group of miners use high-powered hoses at a hydraulic mine site.*

ENTREPRENEURS OF THE GOLD RUSH

Many miners never returned to their homes in the East. Ashamed that they had not made the fortunes they had anticipated, they stayed in California. Most people who came hunting for gold found nothing. Yet others made a lot of money without even searching for gold. These were the people who began their own businesses, providing goods and services to the miners. They were called entrepreneurs.

Two such men were Henry Wells and William Fargo. Both men were from the East. Wells was born in Thetford, Vermont, in 1805. Fargo was born in Pompey, New York, in 1818.

Henry Wells was the son of a clergyman. Though he was born in Vermont, he moved to New York at the age of eight. When he was 22, Wells opened a school for children with speech difficulties. Wells himself had had a stuttering problem. In 1836, Wells began working as a freight agent. He opened his own express freight company in the 1840s.

William Fargo was the oldest of 12 children. He began working as a mail carrier in his hometown at the age of 13. In 1841, he was

Portrait of Henry Wells

A Wells Fargo American Express office in 1866

hired as the first freight agent of Auburn, New York. Fargo eventually went to work for Henry Wells as a messenger. He later became a partner to Wells. He managed all express operations west of Buffalo, New York.

Wells and Fargo formed American Express in 1850. Wells was the company's president until 1868. During that time, many Americans had gone west in search of gold. Wells and Fargo realized that they could make a lot of money by offering banking services to these people.

The other owners of American Express didn't want to head west. Wells, Fargo, and those who believed in them headed west anyway. They formed their own company, called Wells Fargo, on March 18, 1852. The company bought gold dust from miners and provided banking services for the people of California. Wells Fargo banks still provide banking services to people across the nation today.

After the miners traded gold for money at the bank, they needed to buy supplies. One of the most important was food. Philip Danforth Armour recognized this need. Armour was born in upstate New York in 1833.

Armour was a butcher. He moved to California during the gold rush. In California, he set up a meat shop in the city of Placerville. By the age of 24, Armour had made more than $8,000. That was a lot of money at the time. Armour relocated to Wisconsin and used this money to open a meatpacking plant in Milwaukee. He later moved to Chicago, Illinois. There, Armour continued his meatpacking business.

Armour was a pioneer in meat processing. He was one of the first people to use an assembly line. Armour organized his workers so that each had a specific job in butchering the pig. As the pig moved along the assembly line, each

Philip Danforth Armour

worker did his or her specific job. Before this system, each person butchered a pig from start to finish, without help from anyone else. Armour's assembly-line system was much faster. Armour died of pneumonia in 1901. His company was already established as one of the largest hotdog producers in the country.

Besides food, miners also needed to buy clothing. Levi Strauss took advantage of this market. Strauss was born in Bavaria. He came to San Francisco in 1850. Strauss had worked as a tailor. When he came to California, he expected to make a living by making and selling tents and wagon covers. But the sale of these items was not as profitable as Strauss had hoped. He did not attract a lot of customers. Strauss decided to use the canvas he had to make durable pants.

The miners loved the pants Strauss made. Because they were made of a strong material, the pants were perfect for the miners' hard work. People bought the pants as fast as Strauss could make them. Strauss died in San Francisco in 1902. The pants he created, or Levi's jeans, remain popular today.

Miners also needed to buy other equipment. Leland Stanford was a well-known politician who came from a wealthy family. In addition to his political career, he made enormous sums of money by selling equipment to the gold miners.

Stanford was best known as one of the "Big Four." This group also included Mark Hopkins, Collis Huntington, and Charles Crocker. These four men helped build the eastern-bound section of the transcontinental railroad. Stanford was the governor of California. His political influence helped the group get the funding necessary to build the railroad.

Stanford and his wife built a university in honor of their son, who had died in 1884 at age 15. They called it Leland Stanford Junior University. Stanford University is still in operation today.

In addition to these large businesses, other entrepreneurs made money on a smaller scale. A man named John Studebaker made and sold wheelbarrows in Placerville, California. His family eventually used the fortune he made from wheelbarrow sales to make cars.

Lucy Stoddard Wakefield left her husband and went to California during the gold rush. While she was there, she went into business selling pies. She made 240 pies a week. She was able to make a living by selling each pie for one dollar.

Many of the miners who came to California during the gold rush with dreams of becoming rich ended up penniless. But many entrepreneurs were able to take advantage of the gold rush in ways other than mining for gold. And many became very rich.

THE ENTREPRENEURS

Many entrepreneurs made money in the gold rush because they could demand high prices for their goods and services. When the discovery of gold was announced, San Francisco businessman Sam Brannan bought every pan, pick, and shovel he could find. A pan used to cost 20¢, but now Brannan charged $15 for the same pan. He made $36,000 in nine weeks from selling mining equipment.

Gold miners

THE END
OF THE ROAD

The gold rush in California affected people all across the nation. By the end, it seemed as though every person in the country had been a part of it. If a person hadn't gone to California, chances were that a member of his or her family had gone. In the two years following James Marshall's historic discovery of gold, more than 90,000 people made their way to California. By 1854, more than 300,000 people had migrated to California. That was about one out of every 90 people living in the United States.

California's population was forever changed by the gold rush. California became known as a state of risk takers, of people who weren't afraid to fail. Before the discovery of gold, California competed with the other western states, such as Oregon, for settlers. Once James Marshall found gold, California had more people than it could possibly handle. A population survey in 1860 showed that 308,000 people lived in California. That was nearly three times the state's population in 1847.

However, the California gold rush also had negative effects. Most were environmental damage due to hydraulic mining. It destroyed the rivers by diverting their waters to cut away the mountainsides.

Hydraulic mining on mountaintops created problems for people living at the base of the mountains. The earth that was knocked loose

Opposite page: An 1851 map of California's gold region

A NEW MAP OF THE
GOLD REGION
IN
CALIFORNIA
BY
CHARLES DRAYTON GIBBES.
From his own and other
Recent Surveys & Explorations.

from the mountainsides clogged up the streams and rivers that ran below. It became difficult for the rivers to carry overflow floodwater. This created flooding problems. Because the rivers could not hold excess water, there was no way to safely route floodwater away from the cities. Additional silt and sand spread across farmlands in the area. This killed farmers' crops.

Hydraulic mining also led to landslides. Victims of the landslides launched a series of state and federal lawsuits against the mining industry. These lawsuits led to the end of the hydraulic mining industry.

Another negative impact of the California gold rush was to the state's Native American population. Native Americans had been aware of gold in California for hundreds of years. But they did not care about gold. In their society, it had no value. White miners who came to California placed a high value on gold. Native Americans understood this. Some decided to work for the miners.

The miners did not always appreciate the Native Americans' hard work. Many miners believed it would be easy to take advantage of the Native Americans and their knowledge of where to find gold. Some miners took over the Native Americans' dig sites. They stole the gold from the Native Americans, and in some cases even killed them.

The Native Americans had tremendous problems coping with the huge influx of settlers and the resulting changes to their environment. In the first 100 years that the Europeans and the native Californians lived together, 90 percent of the Native American population died. By 1900, California's Native American population was reduced from 300,000 to 16,000.

A Native American settlement in California during the gold rush

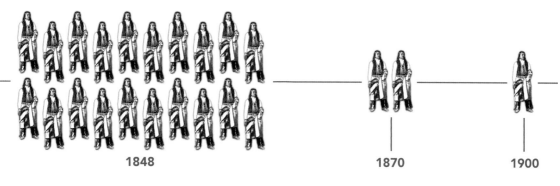

1848   1870   1900

Year	1848	1854	1860	1870	1880	1890	1900
Native Americans	300,000	150,000	67,000	30,000	25,000	19,000	16,000
American Settlers	13,000	300,000	380,000	560,000	865,000	1,213,000	1,485,000

The gold rush nearly wiped out the Native American population in California.

 = 15,000 Native Americans

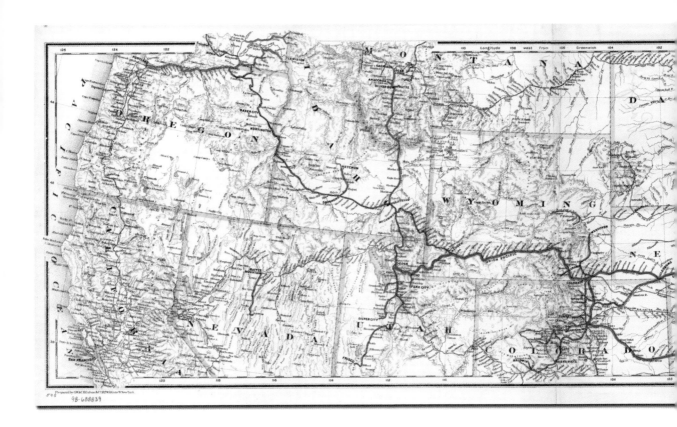

The gold rush also created transportation problems. People were migrating from one side of the nation to the other. So Americans no longer lived solely on the East Coast, but on the West Coast as well. However, there were no airplanes or automobiles. And, people needed an easier way to travel back and forth from both coasts. So, the government had to find a way to connect the nation's population.

In 1853, Congress ordered Secretary of War Jefferson Davis to look into constructing a transcontinental railroad. This kind of railroad runs from one side of a country to the other. President Abraham Lincoln signed the Pacific Railroad Act on July 1, 1862. This act committed the government to help build the railroad.

The government hired two companies to build the transcontinental railroad. They were the Union Pacific and Central Pacific companies.

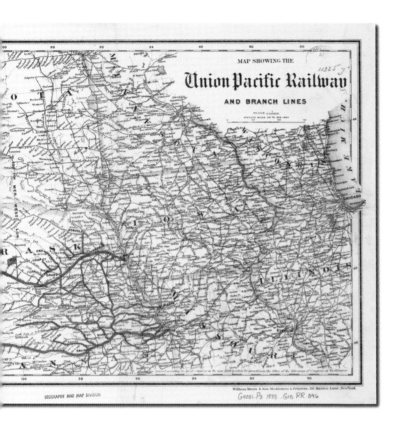

Above: *Jefferson Davis*

Left: *A map of the Union Pacific Railroad*

Union Pacific began building its railroad near Omaha, Nebraska. This railroad traveled west through the Great Plains. Central Pacific began its portion of the railroad in Sacramento, California. This railroad traveled eastward. The Central Pacific railroad went through the Sierra Nevada. The meeting point for the two railroads was the city of Promontory, Utah.

The government promised these companies land grants and money to build the railroad. The amount of money each company received depended on how much of the railroad it built. This influenced both companies to work fast. Both companies used Chinese immigrants and Civil War veterans to build the railroads. The two railroads met in Utah on May 10, 1869. The gold rush had come to an end, but the modernization of the West had just begun.

TIMELINE

1533 Spaniard Hernán Cortés sends a ship to explore the west coast of Mexico.

1542 Juan Rodríguez Cabrillo leads an expedition to San Diego Bay in search of the Strait of Anián. He and his crew are the first Europeans to visit what is now California.

1769 to 1821 California is under Spanish control.

1821 Mexico wins its independence from Spain; California falls under Mexican control.

1841 The first group of American settlers arrives in California.

1847 John Sutter sends James Marshall to build a sawmill on the American River.

1848 On January 24, Marshall discovers gold.

1849 The gold rush is full-blown. About 100,000 people emigrate to California in search of gold.

1850 California becomes part of the United States on September 9.

1869 On May 10, the transcontinental railroad is completed.

1880 Chinese people make up 22 percent of California's miners.

American Moments

FAST FACTS

California is believed to have been named for an island in a sixteenth-century Spanish book. The book is titled *Las Sergas de Esplandián*. The title means "The Exploits of Esplandián."

Thirsty gold seekers in the desert paid high prices for a glass of water. Businessmen took barrels of water to the desert east of California. These businessmen found they could charge desperate forty-niners $1, $5, or $100 for a glass of water.

A man named Rufus Porter wanted to fly people to California during the gold rush. He designed a propeller-driven balloon to transport people. Two hundred people agreed to ride it to California. Porter's idea, however, never became a reality.

In 1850, California imposed a Foreign Miners' Tax. The tax required all miners from other countries to pay $20 per month.

At Promontory, Utah, a golden spike was driven into the ground to commemorate the completion of the transcontinental railroad. Leland Stanford had the honor of hitting the spike. As governor of California, Stanford had helped get the railroad built.

Philip Danforth Armour's use of the assembly line in meatpacking had an important influence. Later, Henry Ford used this production method to make Model T cars.

WEB SITES
WWW.ABDOPUB.COM

Would you like to learn more about the California Gold Rush? Please visit **www.abdopub.com** to find up-to-date Web site links about the California Gold Rush and other American moments. These links are routinely monitored and updated to provide the most current information available.

California gold

GLOSSARY

Baja California Peninsula: a peninsula in Mexico, directly below the state of California. It is surrounded by the Pacific Ocean and the Gulf of California.

Bavaria: a state in southern Germany.

boom: to experience a rapid expansion or increase.

Great Plains: an area of grassy land between the Rocky Mountains and the Mississippi River.

Guaycura Indians: an Indian tribe whose people lived in the California region before the arrival of Europeans.

Mexican War: a war fought between the United States and Mexico between 1846 and 1848.

Oregon Trail: a land route to the western United States extending from various cities on the Missouri River to Oregon, used by miners on their way to California during the gold rush.

Panama Canal: a human-made, narrow canal across Panama that connects the Atlantic and Pacific oceans.

Sierra Nevada: a mountain range in eastern California.

tanner: a person whose business is tanning hides.

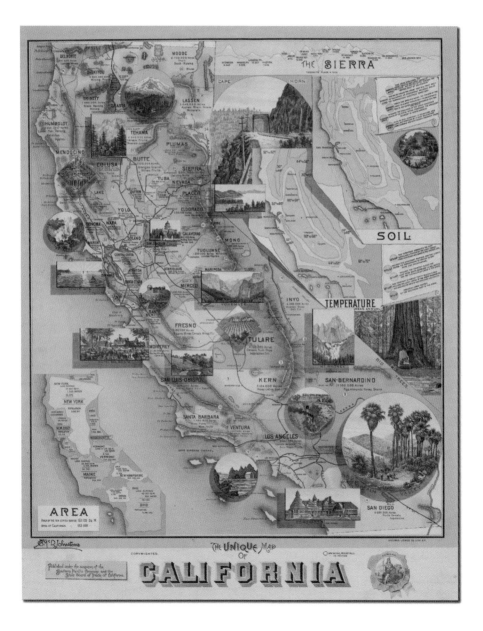

INDEX